THIS BOOK IS TO BE RETURNED

THIS WALKER BOOK BELONGS TO:

_____

_____

_____

_____

First published 1991 by
Walker Books Ltd, 87 Vauxhall Walk
London SE11 5HJ

This edition published 1993

2 4 6 8 10 9 7 5 3

Text © 1991 This selection Jill Bennett
Illustrations © 1991 Graham Percy

Printed in Hong Kong

British Library Cataloguing in Publication Data
A catalogue record for this book is
available from the British Library.

ISBN 0-7445-3040-7

A CUP OF
STARSHINE

poems and pictures for young children

Selected by
Jill Bennett

Illustrated by
Graham Percy

WALKER BOOKS
LONDON

For Baljinder, Poppy and Harpreet,
with thanks for their Little Miss Muffet rhymes.
J.B.

INTRODUCTION

Poetry offers a way of seeing that no other kind of literature can. It can give fresh meaning to the ordinary, everyday experiences of life and illuminate the stranger ones. It tells us about our world in unforgettable words and phrases.

Its music draws children in, delighting their senses, their feelings and their intellects. Rhyme, rhythm and repetition – the 3 Rs of poetry – are especially appealing to young children: they reinforce their aural enjoyment, for poetry needs to be heard to be savoured fully.

The poems I have chosen for this collection range from the ordinary, everyday things like washing, dressing, eating and playing, to stranger ones like the fish with the deep sea smile, the shadow tree, Queen Caroline washing her hair in turpentine and Polly Penwarden painting her toes.

There are poems as well about the sun and the moon, about winter winds and springtime, thunder and rain, fireflies and starshine . . . They come from many different sources, but there is something, I hope, for all moods, places and times:

New sounds to
walk on
today –

Jill R Bennett

WAKE UP

Wake up

Morning
Has
Galloped
Bareback
All night to
Get here

Zaro Weil

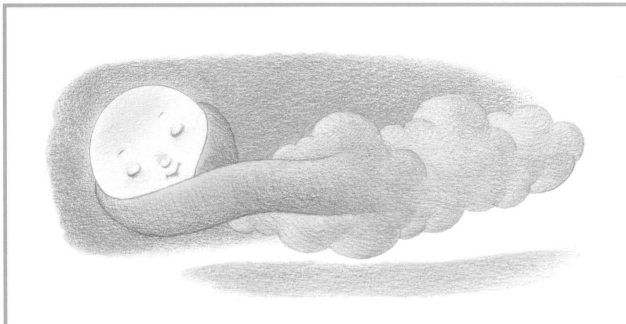

MOON-COME-OUT

Moon-Come-Out
And Sun-Go-In,
Here's a soft blanket
To cuddle your chin.

Moon-Go-In
And Sun-Come-Out,
Throw off the blanket
And bustle about.

Eleanor Farjeon

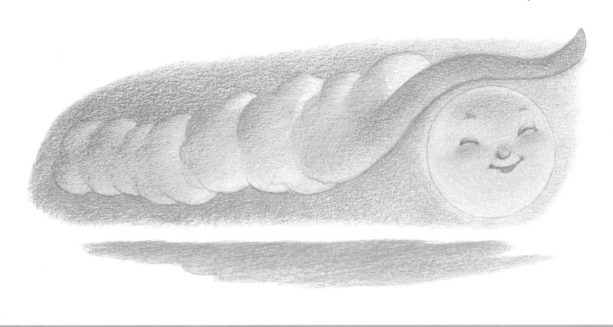

MORNING SONG

Today is a day to catch tadpoles.
Today is a day to explore.
Today is a day to get started.
Come on! Let's not sleep any more.

Outside the sunbeams are dancing.
The leaves sing a rustling song.
Today is a day for adventures,
And I hope that you'll come along!

Bobbi Katz

MONDAY MORNING

Moaning, groaning,
mumbling, grumbling,
glowering, showering,
rubbing, scrubbing,
washing, sploshing,
groping, soaping,
howling, towelling,

splashing, dashing,
muttering, buttering,
crunching, munching,
sighing, tying,
brushing, rushing,
cramming, slamming
and off to
school.

John C. Head

BREAKFAST FOR ONE

Hot thick crusty buttery toast
Buttery toasty thick hot crust
Crusty buttery hot thick toast
Crusty thick hot toasty butter
Thick hot buttery crusty toast
Toasty buttery hot thick crust
Hot buttery thick crusty toast –

with marmalade is how I like it most!

Judith Nicholls

SHADOWS

Chunks of night
Melt
In the morning sun.
One lonely one
Grows legs
And follows me
To school.

Patricia Hubbell

DRINKING FOUNTAIN

When I climb up
   To get a drink,
It doesn't work
   The way you'd think.

I turn it up.
   The water goes
And hits me right
   Upon the nose.

I turn it down
   To make it small
And don't get any
   Drink at all.

Marchette Chute

My shoes are new and squeaky shoes,
They're very shiny, creaky shoes,
I wish I had my leaky shoes
That Mummy threw away.

I liked my old brown leaky shoes
Much better than these creaky shoes,
These shiny, creaky, squeaky shoes
I've got to wear today.

Anon

BIG AND LITTLE

Big boys do,
    Little boys don't.

Big boys will,
    Little boys won't.

Big boys can,
    Little boys can't.

Big boys shall,
    Little boys shan't.

But when little boys
    Are as big as YOU,

Then turn it around
    And it's just as true:

Big boys *don't*,
    Little boys *do*.

William Jay Smith

THE APPLE AND THE WORM

I bit an apple
   That had a worm.
I swallowed the apple,
   I swallowed the worm.
I felt it squiggle,
   I felt it squirm.
I felt it wiggle,
   I felt it turn.
I felt it so slippery,
   Slimy, scummy,
I felt it land – PLOP –
   In my tummy!

I guess that worm is there to stay
Unless . . .
I swallow a bird some day!

Robert Heidbreder

SISTER JILL

When
Sister Jill
has lunch with me
she starts off rather small.

But after lunch
(regretfully)
she ends up
like a
ball.

Gordon Winch

18

THIS TOOTH

I jiggled it
    jaggled it
    jerked it.

I pushed
    and pulled
    and poked it.

But –

As soon as I stopped,
and left it alone,
This tooth came out
on its very own!

Lee Bennett Hopkins

SOMETIMES

Sometimes
when I skip or hop
or when I'm
    jumping

Suddenly
I like to stop
and listen to me
    thumping.

Lilian Moore

POTILO
(a Venda counting song)

Potilo
Hangala
Hangala
Ndatema
Temiso
Tshinoni
Tshagala
Mutanda
Mandule
Guniwee!

NAUGHTY SOAP SONG

Just when I'm ready to
Start on my ears,
That is the time that my
Soap disappears.

It jumps from my fingers and
Slithers and slides
Down to the end of the
Tub, where it hides.

And acts in a most diso-
Bedient way
AND THAT'S WHY MY SOAP'S GROWING
THINNER EACH DAY.

Dorothy Aldis

Why are you under Mummy's bed?
I'm using the springs to scratch my head.
Come out of there and use your own.
I can't do that. The springs are gone.

Ivor Cutler

FULL MOON

Full moon is the nicest time
For telling 'Nancy story
Except the ones 'bout snake and ghost
Because they are so scary

Hide and seek is nice then too
Because it's light as day
And mamas don't say it's too late
If you go out to play

Odette Thomas

A CITY DITTY

Blackout in the buildings,
the big fuse blew;
no electric current,
what will we do?

Can't use the telephone,
can't make toast,
can't use the stereo,
boo, you're a ghost.

Frozen juice cans
getting runny,
frozen meat is
smelling funny.

Traffic signals out
and headlights on the cars,
but what do you know?
We can see the moon and stars.

Eve Merriam

GRANNY GRANNY
PLEASE COMB MY HAIR

Granny Granny
please comb my hair
you always take your time
you always take such care

You put me to sit on a cushion
between your knees
you rub a little coconut oil
parting gentle as a breeze

Mummy Mummy
she's always in a hurry-hurry
rush
she pulls my hair
sometimes she tugs

But Granny
you have all the time in the world
and when you're finished
you always turn my head and say
"Now who's a nice girl."

Grace Nichols

WHO LIKES CUDDLES?

Who likes cuddles?
Me.
Who likes hugs?
Me.

Who likes tickles?
Me.
Who likes getting their face stroked?
Me.
Who likes being lifted up high?
Me.

Who likes sitting on laps?
Me.
Who likes being whirled round and round?
Me.

But best of all I like
getting into bed and getting blowy blowy
down my neck behind my ear.
A big warm tickly blow
lovely.

Michael Rosen

Little Miss Muffet
Sat on her tuffet
Eating a chocolate ice-cream
Along came a spider
Who sat down beside her
And said, "Give me some or I'll scream."

Poppy

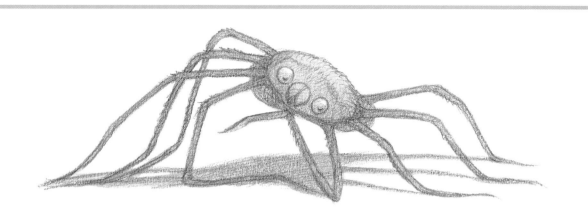

Little Miss Muffet
Sat on her tuffet
Eating her lobster and crabs
Along came a spider
And sat down beside her
And said, "I prefer kebabs."

Baljinder

Little Miss Muffet
Sat on her tuffet
Eating chapatis and chips
Along came a spider
And sat down beside her
And gave her a kiss on the lips.

Harpreet

SKIPPING RHYMES

Salt, mustard, vinegar, pepper
French almond rock,
Bread and butter for your supper
That's all Mother's got.
Fish and chips and Coca Cola,
Pig's head and trout,
Bread and butter for your supper.
O-U-T spells "out".

Anon

Oliver, Oliver, Oliver Twist
I bet you ten dollars you can't do this:
Stand at ease, bend your knees,
Do a quick march, under the arch,
That's not all, drop the ball,
Oliver, Oliver, Oliver Twist.

Anon

Deep in the forest
Where nobody knows
There's a boogy, boogy, boogy
Washing her clothes
With a wish wash there,
And a wish wash here:
That's the way she washes her clothes.
And a boogy, boogy, boogy,
Boogy woo:
That's the way she washes her clothes.

Anon

I know a little boy and he is double jointed
Gave me a kiss and made me disappointed.
Gave me another to match the other,

How many kisses did he give me?
1,2,3,4 . . .

Anon

A DRAGON-FLY

When the heat of the summer
Made drowsy the land,
A dragon-fly came
And sat on my hand,
With its blue jointed body,
And wings like spun glass,
It lit on my fingers
As though they were grass.

Eleanor Farjeon

FIREFLIES

An August night –
    The wind not quite
A wind, the sky
    Not just a sky –
And everywhere
    The speckled air
Of summer stars
    Alive in jars

J. Patrick Lewis

A little yellow cricket
At the roots of the corn
Is hopping about and singing.

Papago Indian

CAMEL

The Camel is a long-legged humpbacked beast
With the crumpled-up look of an old worn shoe.
He walks with a creep and a slouch and a slump
As over the desert he carries his hump
Like a top-heavy ship, like a bumper bump-bump.
See him plodding in caravans out of the East,
Bringing silk for a party and dates for a feast.
Is he tired? Is he *thirsty?* No, not in the least.
Good morning, Sir Camel! Good morning to you!

William Jay Smith

THE ELEPHANT

The elephant goes like this and
That,
He's terribly big and terribly
Fat.
He has no fingers, he has no
Toes,
But goodness, gracious, what a
NOSE!

Anon

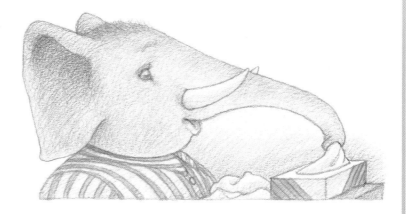

I Wouldn't

There's a mouse house
In the hall wall
With a small door
By the hall floor
Where the fat cat
Sits all day,
Sits that way
All day
Every day
Just to say,
"Come out and play"
To the nice mice
In the mouse house
In the hall wall
With the small door
By the hall floor.

And do they
Come out and play
When the fat cat
Asks them to?

Well, would you?

John Ciardi

At the Farm

What would you say if I said I saw
A hen on the pond and a duck in the straw?

– I think I would say you had best go back
And see if that hen can say, "Quack! Quack!"

When that is done, you may try your luck
At asking that duck to say, "Cluck! Cluck!"

John Ciardi

ROBIN

If on a frosty morning
the robin redbreast calls
his waistcoat red and burning
like a beggar at your walls

throw bread crumbs on the grass for him
when the ground is hard and still
for in his breast there is a flame
that winter cannot kill.

Iain Crichton Smith

THE CAT OF CATS

I am the cat of cats. I am
    The everlasting cat!
Cunning and old, and sleek as jam,
    The everlasting cat!
I hunt the vermin in the night –
    The everlasting cat!
For I see best without the light –
    The everlasting cat!

William Brighty Rands

THE FISH WITH
THE DEEP SEA SMILE

They fished and they fished
Way down in the sea,
Down in the sea a mile.
They fished among all the fish in the sea,
For the fish with the deep sea smile.

One fish came up from the deep of the sea,
From down in the sea a mile,
It had blue-green eyes
And whiskers three
But never a deep sea smile.

One fish came from the deep of the sea,
From down in the sea a mile.
With electric lights up and down his tail,
But never a deep sea smile.

They fished and they fished
Way down in the sea,
Down in the sea a mile.
They fished among all the fish in the sea,
For the fish with a deep sea smile.

One fish came up with terrible teeth,
One fish with long strong jaws,
One fish came up with long stalked eyes,
One fish with terrible claws.

They fished all through the ocean deep,
For many and many a mile.
And they caught a fish with a laughing eye,
But none with a deep sea smile.

And then one day they got a pull,
From down in the sea a mile.
And when they pulled the fish into the boat,
HE SMILED A DEEP SEA SMILE.

And as he smiled, the hook got free,
And then, what a deep sea smile!
He flipped his tail and swam away,
Down in the sea a mile.

Margaret Wise Brown

HIGH ON THE WALL

High on the wall
Where the pennywort grows
Polly Penwarden
Is painting her toes.

One is purple
And two are red
And two are the colour
Of her golden head.

One is blue
And two are green
And the others are the colours
They've always been.

Charles Causley

LITTLE PIPPA

Pip Pip Pippity Pip
Slid on the lino
Slippety Slip
Fell downstairs
Trippety Trip
Tore her knickers
Rippety Rip
Started to cry
Drippety Drip
Poor little Pippa
Pippety Pip.

Spike Milligan

No Harm Done

As I went out
The other day,
My head fell off
And rolled away.

But when I noticed
It was gone,
I picked it up
And put it on.

Anon

Oh, Jemima

Oh, Jemima,
Look at your Uncle Jim!
He's down in the duckpond
Learning how to swim.
First he's on his
Left leg,
Then he's on his
Right –

Now he's on a bar of soap,
Skidding out of
Sight!

Anon

BRIAN O'LIN

Brian O'Lin
Had no breeches to wear
So he bought him a sheepskin
To make him a pair.

With the skinny side out
And the woolly side in
"O, 'tis warm on me bottom!"
Said Brian O'Lin.

Anon

MRS MASON'S BASIN

Mrs Mason bought a basin,
Mrs Tyson said, "What a nice 'un,"
"What did it cost?" said Mrs Frost,
"Half a crown," said Mrs Brown,
"Did it indeed?" said Mrs Reed,
"It did for certain," said Mrs Burton.
Then Mrs Nix up to her tricks
Threw the basin on the bricks.

Anon

Belly and Tubs went out in a boat,
Tubs wore knickers and Belly a coat,
They got in a quarrel and started to shout
And the boat tipped over and they tumbled out.

Clyde Watson

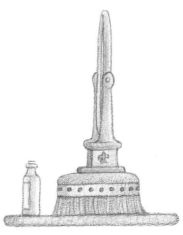

QUEEN CAROLINE

Queen, Queen Caroline,
Washed her hair in turpentine,
Turpentine to make it shine,
Queen, Queen Caroline.

Anon

THE RAINBOW

The rainbow's like a coloured bridge
that sometimes shines from ridge to ridge.
Today one end is in the sea,
the other's in the field with me.

Iain Crichton Smith

AND SUDDENLY SPRING

The winds of March were sleeping.
I hardly felt a thing.
The trees were standing quietly.
It didn't seem like spring.
Then suddenly the winds awoke
And raced across the sky.
They bumped right into April,
Splashing springtime in my eye.

Margaret Hillert

COUNTRY RAIN

The road is full of saucers,
saucers full of rain,
some of them fluted,
some of them plain,
saucers brown as coffee,
saucers full of sky,
saucers full of splashes
as our feet flump by.

Aileen Fisher

THE SHADOW TREE

I'd love to sit
   On the highest branch
But it's much too high
   For me;

So I sit on the grass
   Where the shadow falls,
On the top of
   The shadow tree.

Ilo Orleans

NEW SOUNDS

New sounds to
walk on
today –

dry
leaves,
talking
in hoarse
whispers,
under bare trees.

Lilian Moore

THE MITTEN SONG

"Thumbs in the thumb-place,
Fingers all together!"
This is the song
We sing in mitten-weather,
When it is cold,
It doesn't matter whether
Mittens are wool,
Or made of finest leather –
This is the song
We sing in mitten-weather:
"Thumbs in the thumb-place,
Fingers all together!"

Marie Louise Allen

PENCIL AND PAINT

Winter has a pencil
For pictures clear and neat,
She traces the black tree-tops
Upon a snowy sheet,
But autumn has a palette
And a painting-brush instead,
And daubs the leaves for pleasure
With yellow, brown, and red.

Eleanor Farjeon

I DO NOT MIND YOU, WINTER WIND

I do not mind you, Winter Wind,
when you come whirling by,
to tickle me with snowflakes
drifting softly from the sky.

I do not even mind you
when you nibble at my skin,
scrambling over all of me
attempting to get in.

But when you bowl me over
and I land on my behind,
then I must tell you, Winter Wind,
I mind . . . I really mind!

Jack Prelutsky

WINTER IS A WOLF

Winter is a
    drowsy wolf

full of summer sleep.
He'll awaken and arise
when the hunger in his eyes
grows ravenous and deep.

Winter is a
    clever wolf

You will see him creep
down the wind's way
sly and slow
in a suit of fleecy snow
pretending he's a sheep.

Winter is a
    magic wolf

no man-made cage can keep.
Crouching low on padded paws,
licking his enormous jaws,
earthward he will leap.

Grace Cornell Tall

I TALK WITH THE MOON

I talk with the moon, said the owl
While she lingers over my tree
I talk with the moon, said the owl
And the night belongs to me.

I talk with the sun, said the wren
As soon as he starts to shine
I talk with the sun, said the wren
And the day is mine.

Beverly McLoughland

LISTEN

Shhhhhhhhh!
Sit still, very still
And listen.
Listen to wings
Lighter than eyelashes
Stroking the air.
Know that the high thin breeze
Whispers on high
To the coconut trees.
Listen and hear.

Telcine Turner

IN THE SUN AND SHADOW

The hands of the sun
are warm on me
when I walk in the open meadow,

But the hands feel cool
when I pass a tree
and walk through the leafy shadow.

Aileen Fisher

Don't you ever,
You up in the sky,
Don't you ever get tired
Of having the clouds between
     you and us?

Nootka Indian

SITTING IN THE SAND

Sitting in the sand and the sea comes up
So you put your hands together
And you use them like a cup
And you dip them in the water
With a scooping kind of motion
And before the sea goes out again
You have a sip of ocean.

Karla Kuskin

STARSHINE

I'd like a cup of starshine please
mixed with milk and honey.
And when it comes to soup
can I please
have some that's sunny?

Romesh Gunesekera

RAIN

If you eat lots of carrots
you may see the parrots,
that fly from the moon
before the monsoon
scattering silver rain packets.

Romesh Gunesekera

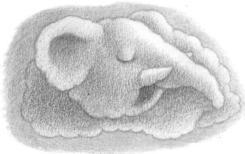

THUNDER

is nothing more
than the roar
of an elephant's snore.

Romesh Gunesekera

THE SWING

The wind blows strong and the swing rides free,
And up in the swing is me, is me,
    And the world goes rushing by,
And one of these days I'll swing so far
I'll go way up where the sea birds are
    And plant my feet on the sky.

Marchette Chute

PAPER BOAT

Make a little paper boat,
Take it to the river,
If it swims and stays afloat
You will live forever.

Gerda Mayer

BEAR

There was a boy
who almost saw
a bear inside
his bed.

O bear, what are
you looking for?
He almost went
and said;

And are you looking
for a boy
that's fat and nicely
fed?

But then he shut
his eyes, and thought
of other things
instead.

Jean Kenward

READING

A story is a special thing.
    The ones that I have read,
They do not stay inside the book,
    They stay inside my head.

Marchette Chute

ROUND AND ROUND

Rosie paints some dark green hills
Under a sky-blue sky,
Rosie paints a red-faced sun,
Some white doves flying high,
Rosie paints a man of straw
Beside the yellow wheat,
Rosie paints some coal black crows
That pick around his feet,
Rosie paints a big, grey cloud,
The cloud begins to rain,
The rain makes all her colours run,
Rosie starts again . . .

Richard Edwards

THROW THE BALL

Let's throw the ball at the sun,
Make it laugh and sigh,
See it hide and smile and run,
Then fall from the evening sky.

Let's throw the ball at the moon,
And watch it falling down,
Then catch it with a silver spoon
In the middle of the town.

Edwin Thumboo

TAKING TURNS

When sun goes home
behind the trees,
and locks her shutters tight –

then stars come out
with silver keys
to open up the night.

Norma Farber

You be saucer,
I'll be cup,
piggyback, piggyback,
pick me up.

You be tree,
I'll be pears,
carry me, carry me
up the stairs.

You be Good,
I'll be Night,
tuck me in, tuck me in
nice and tight.

Eve Merriam

Night-light,
Night-light,
What do you see?
I see you –
Can you see me?

I see a sleepy ceiling,
I see a sleepy floor,
I see soft, sleepy curtains,
I see a sleepy door.

I see a sleepy toy chest,
I see a silent ball,
I see a sleepy picture
Nodding on the wall.

I see a sleepy window,
I see a sleepy chair,
I see a sleepy, sleepy blanket
And a yawning teddy bear.

Night-light,
Night-light,
What do you see?
I see you –
Can you see me?

Eve Merriam

INDEX OF FIRST LINES

INDEX OF POETS

ACKNOWLEDGEMENTS

The editor and publishers gratefully acknowledge permission to reproduce the following copyright material:

"Naughty Soap Song" by Dorothy Aldis; reprinted by permission of G.P. Putnam's Sons from *All Together* by Dorothy Aldis; copyright 1925-1928, 1934, 1939, 1952; copyright renewed 1953-1956, 1962, 1967 by Dorothy Aldis. "The Mitten Song" by Marie Louise Allen; from *A Pocketful of Poems* by Marie Louise Allen, Harper and Row, Publishers, Inc.; copyright © 1957 by Marie Allen Howarth; reprinted by permission of Harper and Row, Publishers, Inc. "This Tooth" © Lee Bennett Hopkins 1970; from *More Surprises*, Harper and Row, Publishers, Inc.; reprinted by permission of Curtis Brown Ltd. "High on the Wall" © Charles Causley 1975; from *Collected Poems*, Macmillan Publishers Ltd; reproduced by permission of David Higham Associates Ltd. "Reading" and "The Swing" by Marchette Chute; from *Rhymes About Us*, E.P. Dutton, Inc.; copyright © 1974 by Marchette Chute; reprinted by permission of Mary Chute Smith. "At the Farm" and "I Wouldn't" by John Ciardi; from *You Read to Me, I'll Read to You*, J.B. Lippincott Co.; copyright © 1962 John Ciardi; reprinted by permission of Harper and Row, Publishers, Inc. "Winter is a Wolf" © Grace Cornell Tall 1985; from *Cricket Magazine*, January 1985, Volume 12, No. 5; reproduced by permission of the author. "Rainbow" and "Robin" © Iain Crichton Smith 1983; from *A Scottish Poetry Book*, Oxford University Press; reproduced by permission of the author. "Why are you under Mummy's bed?" © Ivor Cutler 1991. "Don't You Ever?" (Nootka Indian) from *Nootka and Quilete Music*, Bureau of American Ethnology, Bulletin 24; © Frances Densmore 1939; reproduced by permission of The Smithsonian Institution. "Drinking Fountain" by Marchette Chute; from *Around and About* by Marchette Chute, E.P. Dutton, Inc.; copyright © 1957 by E.P. Dutton, Inc.; copyright renewed 1985 by Marchette Chute; reprinted by permission of Mary Chute Smith. "Round and Round" © Richard Edwards 1987; from *Whispers From a Wardrobe*, Lutterworth Press; reproduced by permission of Lutterworth Press. "Taking Turns" by Norma Farber; reprinted by permission of Coward, McCann & Geoghegan; from *Small Wonders* by Norma Farber, Coward, McCann & Geoghegan; text © 1978 by Norma Farber. "A Dragon-Fly" © Eleanor Farjeon 1981; from *Invitation to a Mouse*, Pelham Books Ltd; reproduced by permission of David Higham Associates Ltd. "Moon-Come-Out" and "Pencil and Paint" © Eleanor Farjeon 1951; from *Silver-Sand and Snow*, Michael Joseph Ltd; reproduced by permission of David Higham Associates Ltd. "Country Rain" and "In the Sun and Shadow" from *Out in the Dark and the Daylight* by Aileen Fisher, Harper and Row, Publishers, Inc.; text copyright © 1980 by Aileen Fisher; reproduced by permission of Harper and Row, Publishers, Inc. "Starshine", "Rain" and "Thunder" © Romesh Gunesekera 1991. "Monday Morning" © John C. Head 1986; from *A First Lick of the Lolly*, Macmillan Education Ltd; reproduced by permission of the author. "The Apple and the Worm" © Robert Heidbreder 1985; from *Don't Eat Spiders*, Oxford University Press; reproduced by permission of Oxford University Press Canada. "And Suddenly Spring" © Margaret Hillert 1972; from *The Sky Is Full Of Song*, Harper and Row, Publishers, Inc.; reproduced by permission of the author, who controls all rights. "Shadows" by Patricia Hubbell; reprinted with permission of Atheneum Publishers, an imprint of Macmillan Publishing Company; from *Catch Me a Wind*, Atheneum Publishers. Copyright © 1968 by Patricia Hubbell. "Big and Little" and "Camel" by William Jay Smith; from *Laughing Time* by William Jay Smith, Delacorte Press, an imprint of Bantam Doubleday Dell Publishing Group Inc.; copyright © 1955, 1957, 1980, 1990 by William Jay Smith; reprinted by permission of Farrar, Straus and Giroux, Inc. "Bear" © Jean Kenward 1974; from *Old Mister Hotchpotch*, Thornhill Press; reproduced by permission of Harper and Row, Publishers, Inc. "Sitting in the Sand" by Karla Kuskin; from *Dogs and Dragons, Trees and Dreams* by Karla Kuskin, Harper and Row, Publishers, Inc.; copyright © 1980 by Karla Kuskin; reproduced by permission of Harper and Row, Publishers, Inc. "Fireflies" © J. Patrick Lewis 1991. "Paper Boat" © Gerda Mayer 1980; from *Monkey on the Analyst's Couch*, Ceolfrith Press; reproduced by permission of the author. "I Talk with the Moon" © Beverly McLoughland 1960; from *More Surprises*, Harper and Row Publishers, Inc.; reproduced by permission of the author. "A City Ditty" © Eve Merriam 1989; from *A Poem for a Pickle*, Morrow Jr. Books, a division of William Morrow and Co., Inc.; reproduced by permission of Marian Reiner for the author. "Night-light" © Eve Merriam 1985; from *Blackberry Ink*, Morrow Jr. Books, a division of William Morrow and Co., Inc.; reproduced by permission of Marian Reiner for the author. "You be Saucer" © Eve Merriam 1988; from *You Be Good and I'll Be Night*, Morrow Jr. Books, a division of William Morrow and Co., Inc.; reproduced by permission of Marian Reiner for the author. "Little Pippa" © Spike Milligan 1963; from *Little Pot Boiler*, Dobson Books Ltd; reproduced by permission of Spike Milligan Productions Ltd. "New Sounds" © Lilian Moore 1975; from *Little Racoon and Other Poems from the Woods*, Atheneum Publishers, an imprint of Macmillan Publishing Company; reproduced by permission of Marian Reiner for the author. "Sometimes" © Lilian Moore 1967; from *I Feel the Same Way*, Atheneum Publishers, an imprint of Macmillan Publishing Company; reproduced by permission of Marian Reiner for the author. "A Little Yellow Cricket" (Papago Indian); from *Singing for Power: The Song Magic of the Papago Indians of Southern Arizona* by Ruth Murray Underhill, The University of California Press; copyright © Ruth Murray Underhill, 1938, 1966; reproduced by permission of The University of California Press. "Breakfast for One" © Judith Nicholls 1986; from *A First Lick of the Lolly*, Macmillan Education Ltd; reproduced by permission of the author. "Granny Granny Please Comb My Hair" © Grace Nichols 1984; from *Come Into My Tropical Garden*, A. and C. Black; reproduced by permission of Curtis Brown Ltd on behalf of the author. "I Do Not Mind You, Winter Wind" © Jack Prelutsky 1984; from *It's Snowing! It's Snowing!* by Jack Prelutsky, Greenwillow Books, a division of William Morrow and Co., Inc.; reproduced by permission of Greenwillow Books. "Morning Song" by Bobbi Katz; from *Poems for Small Friends* by Bobbi Katz, Random House, Inc.; copyright © Random House, Inc. 1989; reproduced by permission of the author. "Who Likes Cuddles?" © Michael Rosen 1985; from *Don't Put Mustard in the Custard*, Andre Deutsch Ltd; reproduced by permission of Andre Deutsch Ltd. "The Fish With the Deep Sea Smile" by Margaret Wise Brown; from *Nibble Nibble* by Margaret Wise Brown, Harper and Row, Publishers, Inc.; copyright © William R. Scott, Inc. 1959; © renewed by Roberta Brown Rauch 1987; reprinted by permission of Harper and Row, Publishers, Inc. "Full Moon" © Odette Thomas 1975; from *Rain Falling, Sun Shining*, Bogle-L'Ouverture Publications; reproduced by permission of Bogle-L'Ouverture Publications. "Throw the Ball" © Edwin Thumboo 1988; from *My Blue Poetry Book*, Macmillan Education Ltd; reproduced by permission of the author. "Listen" © Telcine Turner 1977; from *Song of the Surreys*, Macmillan, London and Basingstoke; reproduced by permission of Macmillan, London and Basingstoke. "Belly and Tubs Went Out in a Boat" by Clyde Watson; from *Father Fox's Pennyrhymes* by Clyde Watson, Harper and Row, Publishers, Inc.; copyright © Clyde Watson 1971; reproduced by permission of Harper and Row, Publishers, Inc. "Venda Counting Song" from *Venda Children's Songs* by John Blacking, Witwatersrand University Press 1967. Published with permission. © Witwatersrand University Press. "Wake Up!" © Zaro Weil 1989; from *Mud, Moon and Me*, Orchard Books, a division of The Watts Group; reproduced by kind permission of Orchard Books, 96 Leonard Street, London EC2A 4RH. "Sister Jill" © Gordon Winch 1984; from *Popcorn and Porcupines*, Hodder and Stoughton Australia; reproduced by permission of Hodder and Stoughton Australia.

While every effort has been made to obtain permission, there may still be cases in which we have failed to trace a copyright holder, and we would like to apologize for any apparent negligence.

MORE WALKER PAPERBACKS
For You to Enjoy

OUT AND ABOUT
by Shirley Hughes

Eighteen richly illustrated poems portray the weather and activities associated with the various seasons.

"Hughes at her best. Simple, evocative rhymes conjure up images that then explode in the magnificent richness of her paintings." *The Guardian*

0-7445-1422-3   £3.99

OVER THE MOON
A Book of Nursery Rhymes
illustrated by Charlotte Voake

"A lovely book, this; well over a hundred rhymes, familiar and less so, with blithe and airy pictures."
Naomi Lewis, The Observer

0-7445-1372-3   £5.99

WHEN DAD CUTS DOWN THE CHESTNUT TREE
WHEN DAD FILLS IN THE GARDEN POND
by Pam Ayres/Graham Percy

Two affectionate rhyming texts on a conservationist theme. The advantages and disadvantages of a chestnut tree and a garden pond come under a child's scrutiny.

When Dad Cuts Down the Chestnut Tree   0-7445-1436-3
When Dad Fills in the Garden Pond   0-7445-1437-1
£3.99 each